ROAD

This book is dedicated to the memory of my grandmother, Doreen O'Connor, a fantastic sportswoman in her own right, who never missed a single game I played.

AB de Villiers

ROAD TO GLORY

Jeremy Daniel

Jonathan Ball Publishers
Cape Town & Johannesburg

Text and illustrations © Jonathan Ball Publishers 2018
Published edition © Jonathan Ball Publishers 2018

Originally published in South Africa in 2018 by
JONATHAN BALL PUBLISHERS
A division of Media24 (Pty) Ltd
PO Box 33977
Jeppestown
2043

ISBN 978-1-86842-862-5
ebook ISBN 978-1-86842-863-2

Every effort has been made to trace the copyright holders and to obtain their permission for the use of copyright material. The publishers apologise for any errors or omissions and would be grateful to be notified of any corrections that should be incorporated in future editions of this book.

Twitter: www.twitter.com/JonathanBallPub
Facebook: www.facebook.com/JonathanBallPublishers
Blog: http://jonathanball.bookslive.co.za/

Edited by Liz Sparg
Proofread by Paul Wise
Cover by Johan Koortzen
Design, typesetting and illustrations by Johan Koortzen
Set in 13 on 18pt Bembo Std

Printed by **novus print**.a Novus Holdings company

Contents

CHAPTER 1

NEW WORLD RECORDS

AB hopped over the boundary rope and onto the field, grinning at the sight and sound of a packed Wanderers Stadium. He swung his bat from side to side and listened to the crowd roaring his name, 'AB, AB, AB!'

It took him a moment to adjust to the fact that most of the people at the Proteas' one-day international against the West Indies were dressed in bright pink with green trimmings. So was he, under his black pads and helmet.

It was Pink Day, 18 January 2015 – a day when people across South Africa raised funds and awareness for breast cancer – and the atmosphere was amazing.

His thoughts turned quickly to the game. It was one of those crisp, still Highveld afternoons, clear for kilometres around, and the openers had provided the perfect setup. Hashim Amla and Rilee Rossouw had each made a century and it was only the 35th over. The score was 247 runs for one wicket.

Just a few days earlier, the West Indies had chased down a massive T20 score of 232 runs to beat the Proteas, and AB knew that they were still feeling confident. But today his team had a chance to strike back.

A series against the men from the Caribbean was always an epic encounter. During the years of apartheid, when South Africa was banned from playing international sport, the West Indies had dominated world cricket. Names like Viv Richards, Malcolm Marshall and Brian Lara would always be legendary. But that was a long time ago, and this year the West Indies team was rebuilding. AB knew they were beatable and tonight was a good night to do it.

Taking guard, he studied the gaps in the field and then focused all his attention on fast bowler Jerome Taylor. The first ball was straight, full and slower – meant to trick him into playing early. AB opened his stance, paused for a beat, and swung straight. He didn't connect perfectly, but the ball raced past the bowler and just beat the outfield for four. The crowd roared and AB relaxed a little; he was off the mark. Two more quiet deliveries helped him settle and get his eye in, then the next one sat up perfectly and AB swiped it back to the boundary for four more.

By the end of the over, AB had 18 runs behind his name and a familiar relaxed feeling washed over him. Was this going to be one of those nights when everything went his way?

The next ball was slightly overpitched, so he moved across his stumps and hooked it for six. It was a huge hit, landing just under the Wanderers scoreboard. The kids in the stands charged around looking for the ball, to claim it as a prize before throwing it back to the fielder.

AB decided he would take a few chances today. A scoop and pull over his shoulder sent the next ball sailing for another six, and the Wanderers crowd went crazy.

AB looked across at Hashim Amla batting

3

alongside him. Hashim shook his head in amusement and gave AB a thumbs-up. AB and Hash had been playing in the same games for so many years that no words were needed. AB knew that Hash wanted him to push the score along.

He also knew that he had the fierce support of his coach and that a top-quality line-up of batsmen was waiting in the dressing room, if anything went wrong. He decided to take his foot off the brake and see what would happen.

In came Andre Russell, who bowled a full toss, and AB dispatched it for six more runs. Another full toss, six more … and suddenly AB was on 52 runs after only 16 deliveries. The stadium announcer's voice cut through the deafening cheers.

'A massive Wanderers hand for the fastest 50 in a one-day international in history! The one and only AB de Villiers!'

AB couldn't believe it – 50 runs in only 16 balls. Hash came jogging over and embraced him.

'What's up with you, Abbas? You're on fire!' Hash exclaimed, as AB raised his bat to the cheering crowd and nodded to the dressing room.

'Just my lucky day, I guess,' replied AB. 'But I'm going to try for a few more.'

'No doubt,' said Hashim, as he jogged back to his crease.

AB knew that many people called him the best one-day cricketer in the world. Some days it made him proud, and on other days he felt he wasn't worthy of that title. But now he had a world record behind his name. He was captain of the Proteas and the number one batsman in the world, and this was his moment.

Then the celebrations of his half-century were over and it was time to get back to business. AB got into his groove, knocking a few singles around, batting some boundaries, and, every few balls, unleashing a mighty six. He was feeling invincible, until a short, angry delivery from Taylor cut back at him, narrowly missing the stumps.

'Watch out, AB,' the wicketkeeper warned. 'You've made him angry now.'

'Luck is running out, mister,' said another voice from the slips, but AB kept his eyes firmly forward and focused on what he wanted to do.

Reverse sweeps, drives, square cuts; they were all working to perfection and the West Indies had no reply.

At 92 runs off 29 balls, he moved right across his stumps, got down on one knee and hoisted the ball miles over mid-wicket for six. AB had scored 98 runs from only 30 balls and the crowd was going wild. This was it.

AB met Hash in the middle of the pitch and they bumped fists.

'I don't think that last one has even landed yet,' said Hash, and AB chuckled. 'One more and that's the fastest century ever,' Hash continued.

'*Ja,*' AB agreed. 'Better get back to work'.

As Jason Holder, the all-rounder, turned and walked back to his mark for the next ball, AB noticed that he was wearing the number 98 on his back. Surely that was a sign that this was his day?

Holder steamed in and bowled. AB saw the ball as big and beautiful as a grapefruit. Feeling like he had all the time in the world, he crashed it over mid-wicket and into the crowd for six. A century off only 31 balls: another world record.

All the tension flowed out of AB's body and he burst out laughing, then walked straight into a bear hug from his teammate. It doesn't get better than this, he thought. At the same time, his mind flashed back to the years of hard work and struggle, the highs and lows of a sporting career and how it had all begun.

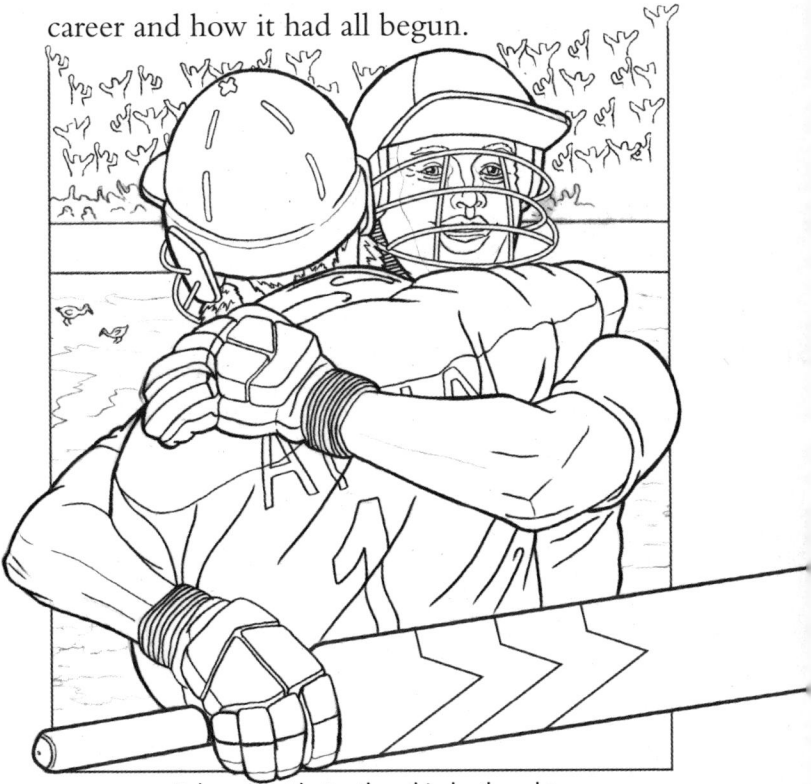

It doesn't get better than this, he thought.

CHAPTER 2

THE FIGHTER

AB stood barefoot and shivering, straining his eyes to see what was happening. Because he was only 11 years old, he had been placed far on the square leg boundary, which was almost out in the street.

His mother called them for dinner – for the third time – but this was a very important moment in the game. He was playing cricket with his two older brothers, Jan and Wessels and their best friend, Gerrit Deist. Even though AB's stomach was rumbling and his feet were numb with cold, dinner would have to wait.

AB heard Jan motoring in and bowling, then saw the flash of a bat and heard the taped-up tennis ball making contact.

'Catch!' shouted Jan.

Every nerve in AB's body went on high alert.

But the gathering gloom made it nearly impossible to see. He saw a dark flash and hurled himself to his left, arms outstretched. The ball sank into his hands.

'Got him! I got him!' shouted AB, jumping to his feet, and Jan whooped and clapped while Wessel threw down his bat in disgust.

'You're a legend, kid! For an 11-year-old that was one amazing catch,' Wessels grinned, and AB beamed with pride. There was no higher praise than from his older brothers.

'Can I bat now?' he asked. 'It's my turn.'

'Nah, let's call it quits for the night. Floodlights aren't working,' joked Gerrit.

'I don't care,' said AB quickly. 'I can see fine. And it's my turn. I caught him.'

The older boys paused and looked at each other. Jan shrugged.

'OK, I guess you deserve a few balls. But we're not going easy on you just 'cos you're a *laaitie*.'

AB grinned. He reached down for Gerrit's bat and remembered how it was much too heavy for him.

Gerrit laughed. 'He can barely lift it. This shouldn't take long.'

'*Ja*. One more ball then we're coming, ma,' shouted Jan as the three older boys laughed and took up their positions.

Gerrit was in his early twenties and the fastest bowler in town. But AB was desperate to prove that he deserved to play. He needed to prove he was a fighter. He gritted his teeth and took up his stance in front of the wicket, deciding to rest the heavy bat on top of the wicket, so that he wouldn't have to do a full backlift.

The first ball caught him high up on the thigh before he even saw it. It stung sharply, but AB said nothing, just threw the ball back to Gerrit and tried to rub his leg without anyone noticing. The next one he spotted early and blocked, then picked it up and threw it back to the bowler.

'Boys! Your food's getting cold and I'm not asking again,' shouted his mother from inside.

'Stop messing around, Gerrit. Bowl him,' said Wessels.

AB was getting colder and hungrier by the minute, but more than anything else, he was determined. Ten deliveries later, he was still defending his wicket in the almost pitch darkness.

'*Ag*, come guys, let's go inside. I can't get him out,' said Gerrit.

'AB carries his bat into tomorrow's game,' announced Jan, and his brothers clapped as AB walked off.

Nothing had ever sounded sweeter to AB's ears than the sound of that clapping.

CHAPTER 3

THE FIRST WORLD CUP

AB was dreaming deeply when a hand reached under the covers and started shaking him.

'AB, wake up. Wake up, man! It's started.'

For a few seconds, he felt groggy and confused, but suddenly he remembered. It was the 1992 Cricket World Cup in Australia and South Africa was playing Pakistan. He bolted out of bed and rushed down to the lounge where the rest of the family were gathered around the television.

South Africa had never before competed in a Cricket World Cup, and the whole nation was gripped by every twist and turn of the tournament. On Protea match days, life in the De Villiers house ground to a halt.

AB sat on the couch, pulled a blanket up under his chin and thanked his mom for the steaming hot chocolate that she handed to him. Because of the time difference between Australia and South Africa, the games started in the middle of the night and the whole family would be exhausted for the rest of the day. But they never skipped a game.

The South Africans had lost the toss and been put in to bat by Pakistan. They had managed 211 runs in their 50 overs, Andrew Hudson top scoring with 54 runs. Then the rain had come down and changed the maths; now their opponents only needed to score 194 runs off 36 overs to win.

Pakistan reached 50 runs without a loss before Richard Snell clean bowled Aamer Sohail and brought Inzamam-ul-Haq, nicknamed 'Inzy', to the wicket. AB was nervous; Inzy was a massive hitter and he could chase down any total if he got going.

'I told you Snell was the man,' said Jan. 'You're always moaning about him.'

'Let's wait and see,' AB replied. 'This game's not over yet.'

AB's worst fears started to come true, as Inzy laid into the South African attack. The De Villiers family fell silent.

'Are you still awake in there?' AB's mom asked from the kitchen, but no one bothered to reply.

On 48 runs, Inzy tapped one down and started off for a quick single. Jonty Rhodes accelerated from point, and suddenly Inzy realised he was in trouble. He stopped, turned and tried to get back into his crease. Jonty bent down and scooped up the ball, not even breaking his stride.

AB jumped off the couch and watched in absolute disbelief as Jonty decided not to throw at the stumps, but instead accelerated his run and then launched his body at full stretch, demolishing the stumps in front of him and running the danger-man out!

'Wooooooooo! Did you see that?' screamed AB, but everyone was already up on their feet. The television replayed the run out over and over again, and it just kept looking better. It was the turning point in the game and the South Africans won by 20 runs.

The exciting game fed AB's taste for high-stakes competition. It also made him realise that he'd been so focused on his batting that he had neglected his fielding. Jonty Rhodes was his new hero and he decided to start practising his fielding every single day, until he was as skilled as Jonty.

CHAPTER 4

THE TRICKSTER

When he heard the doorbell ring, AB jumped up and shot to the front door. His parents were having a braai and had invited a few friends over for a long, lazy afternoon.

The boys chatted to the grownups, until, released at last, they raced each other to the 'B field', a cramped square of cracked concrete behind the house, where the washing line and neighbours' wall were fielders and the bathroom door was the wicket.

When the 'A field' was busy at the De Villiers' Mentz Avenue home, the action moved to the 'B field', a much more challenging pitch. The 'A field' was the wide, green front lawn that opened up onto the street, but the 'B field' was small, enclosed and grassless.

The crack that ran through its concrete slab

always attracted bowlers. They aimed to pitch the ball right at it and then hooted with laughter as it shot off in different directions, often straight at the batsman's head.

'One hand, one bounce,' announced Wessels, and everyone nodded.

'Kitchen door is out, and the wall with no bounce is four,' said AB.

AB was put in to bat first, and the others gathered in close, half hoping to take a great catch and half hoping to avoid a ball speeding towards them.

'Come on AB, let's see what you've got today!' shouted Jan, as AB squared up.

AB loved batting on the B field, because it threw up challenges that he handled better than the older boys he was playing with. He had spent hours there on his own, bouncing the ball off the walls and then trying out various hooks, pulls, cuts and sweeps, depending on how the ball behaved.

He was ready for anything.

The first ball hit the crack perfectly, then

skidded straight on under AB's outstretched bat, before narrowly missing the stumps, then bouncing off the wall and into the back of AB's head. Everyone laughed, even AB.

'That was unplayable,' he said, 'Even Clive Rice would have missed it.'

'Excuses, excuses,' muttered the other boys.

The music started up inside and they smelled the boerewors fat as it hit the hot coals of the braai. For the next ball, AB lifted his bat and prepared to drive, until suddenly the ball hit a stone and changed direction. In a flash, AB adjusted his stance, twisted and launched the ball over the wall and into the neighbour's garden.

There was a stunned silence at first, and then everyone burst out laughing and rushed over to high five him.

'AB, how did you change your shot so fast?' asked Wessels. 'That was insane. If you keep that up, you'll be playing for South Africa in the next World Cup.'

AB was pleased. To him, his moves seemed natural. He didn't even have to think about them.

In a flash, AB adjusted his stance and launched the ball over the wall.

But he liked how much other people enjoyed watching him play, and he couldn't wait to think up some more trick shots to show his friends.

'Come on, let's keep going! You'll never get me out,' he shouted.

'One problem, pal,' said his brother. 'You just hit our last ball into a garden three houses down from here.'

CHAPTER 5

TEST MATCH

AB felt his dad's powerful arms wrap around his waist and lift him into the air, above the heads of the family walking in front of him. As he looked around the inside of a Test cricket ground for the first time, he knew he would never forget this moment.

It was the second morning of the first Test against England, 17 November 1995. The males of the De Villiers family had driven two hours from their home in Warmbaths to Centurion, laughing and singing all the way. And now they were here.

AB took in the feel of the stadium: the smells of braais, sunscreen and beer so early in the morning, the sounds of laughter and cheering, kids running around, moms setting up blankets and cushions on the grass and everyone looking forward to a full day of cricket.

Looking around at the crowd, AB spotted his brothers jumping up and down and waving to him and his father.

'Dad, Dad, over there,' he shouted and pointed. 'They've got a *lekker* spot on the grass.'

AB was stepping carefully over a picnic basket, when a cheer went up from the crowd and he turned to see his heroes jogging onto the field. The awesome Allan Donald, shrewd captain Hansie Cronje, legendary all-rounder Brian McMillan, right here in the flesh. AB knew all of them and what their roles were in the team.

'AB, come, let's go down to the boundary, see if we can get an autograph or something,' Jan suggested.

'OK, hang on, coming,' he replied and reached into his bag for the bat he planned to use at lunchtime on the field. It would be fantastic to cover it with players' signatures.

Behind him AB could see the two English opening batsmen through the dressing room window, nodding and listening to a coach who was speaking urgently to them. On the field, the Proteas were huddled in a semi-circle, with their arms around each other. AB guessed they were praying. In the stands, the atmosphere was electric, as everyone waited for the game to start.

The Protea players leaned into the circle, broke out and took up their fielding positions. Allan Donald jogged off towards the wickets, gave his cap to the umpire and started measuring out his run, while Hansie Cronje studied the ball and shone it by rubbing it on his white trousers.

The game announcer was talking non-stop, but neither AB nor Jan could make out a word of what he was saying. From where they were standing by the mid-wicket boundary, AB watched as Shaun Pollock started running towards them.

'Shaun's making his Test debut today,' said AB.

'I know,' Jan replied. 'He's coming right towards us.'

AB had never been so close to a sports hero before. Pollock came from a legendary cricketing family and was one of the most promising young all-rounders in the world. And here he was, standing on the field just a few metres away from AB.

He's just a normal person, like me, AB thought. That could be me one day, if I work hard and play well.

'Stop daydreaming,' Jan told AB. 'Donald's warming up for the first ball.'

The English captain, Mike Atherton, was going to face the first ball. He settled down in his crease as Allan Donald paced up and down in the outfield, adjusting his grip, then turning quickly and speeding in before hurling down a blisteringly fast ball, outside off stump. Atherton lifted his bat, watched it go by and noted the swing and the bounce of the pitch. Dot ball.

Shaun Pollock turned and came walking back to the boundary.

'Shaun! Hey Shaun!' shouted out Jan, and Pollock turned to look at them. 'Can you sign my brother's bat?'

'Maybe later,' responded Shaun and turned away.

AB grinned as Jan punched him on the arm. Pollock spoke to them!

Watching the Proteas play, AB decided that, one day, he was going to play Test cricket for the South African national team.

CHAPTER 6

HOME ALONE

As the baby in the family, AB had always known that one day his brothers would move out of home and start their own families.

When it happened, he wasn't prepared for it. Of course, there were advantages. For a start, he could change television channels whenever he wanted to.

But AB missed the closeness of brotherhood terribly. The house was so quiet that he started playing his music louder than ever. Plus, all the games in the garden and team sports were reserved for weekend visits, so AB had to get creative.

The first thing he did was sling a rope over a wooden beam in the garage, tie a sock to the rope, and stuff a tennis ball into the sock so that it hung there, ready to be hit. Then he practised driving the ball over and over and over again, until he knew that he could do it in his sleep.

The only thing that AB loved as much as cricket was watching Wimbledon tennis matches on television. During the 1994 tournament, he got his mom's permission to paint a white line on the back wall and that became the centre court tennis net.

He would devour every minute of a match, then race outside during the changeover to serve a few balls against the wall, or try a backhand technique he had just seen on the screen, before racing back inside to catch the start of the next set.

AB even figured out a way to play a full tennis match all by himself. 'Sampras serves,' he shouted out as he smashed a serve into the wall. 'Great return from Agassi! Sampras, Agassi, Sampras … ooh that's a winner … 15–0 to Sampras.'

He tried to keep the solo matches fair, playing his best shots for both players, no matter which one he preferred in real life. But it wasn't always easy.

Although he was a little lonely at home, at school things were going really well. At nursery school, he and his friends Skippy, Stof and Chris had spent their afternoons getting up to mischief in the sleepy town of Warmbaths. When the four buddies ended up in the same class in Standard 2, their friendship got stronger, and AB forgot how much he missed his brothers.

The friends lost themselves in the world of international sports. One minute they were pretending to be professional golfer Tiger Woods, who had just become the youngest ever winner of a Masters Tournament, and the next minute they were re-enacting the moment when Mike Tyson bit off a piece of Evander Holyfield's ear, during a world title boxing match.

In the De Villiers home, cricket was tops, but at school, rugby was on everyone's minds for most of the year. Rugby practice was three times a week, and it quickly became the highlight of AB's week. He had proven himself repeatedly at scrum-half and centre, but he really wanted a chance to shine in his favourite position: fly-half.

CHAPTER 7

GETTING NOTICED

AB lined up on the touchline with the rest of the team – all dressed in crisply ironed uniforms, barefoot, and with their hair neatly brushed – and stared across the field at the opponents. The knot in his stomach tightened like a belt.

'OK boys, this is the big one,' said the coach, pacing up and down in front of them. 'You all know we've struggled against Kruger Park Primary in the past. But this year is going to be different. We've got the players, we're fitter than ever and I can see that you guys are pumped up to get a victory.'

The boys all nodded and AB felt his fear turning to excitement.

Out of the corner of his eye, he spotted a flash of white, and he turned to see his dad getting out of the car and walking towards the field in his doctor's coat.

It was a big moment for AB. His dad was usually busy with patients and couldn't get out in the middle of the day to watch him play. But AB had told his dad what an important game this was and he had managed to come.

The teams took to the field and walked past each other in a long line, shaking hands and sizing each other up. AB had been promoted to the older team, so he was much smaller than the rest of the players. But there was no time to worry about that as the whistle blew and suddenly the game was on.

Both teams played great rugby all through the game, passing cleanly, running straight lines and tackling hard. Towards the end, the game was still tied at five all. Then Warmbaths Primary won a scrum on the 10-metre line.

'Come on boys, this is our last chance,' shouted the captain, and slapped AB on the back.

AB looked over to where his dad was standing, and at his schoolmates, who were doing one of their high-energy war cries in the stands. Then he looked up at the posts, deciding whether he could reach them with a drop kick. It would be about the same as hitting the eucalyptus tree from across the road, on the second branch. If he missed, the game would be over and everyone would blame him.

The scrum set and the ball was fed into it. A huge push, then it popped out to the scrum-half, who grabbed the ball and did a diving pass to AB. He caught the ball cleanly, dropped it softly in front of his bare right foot and kicked. He made contact beautifully and the ball soared high.

Everyone stopped and watched as it reached its highest point, hung there and started dropping. AB suddenly felt sick. He didn't have the distance; it was going to fall short. Or was it?

A roar went up from the stands, the ref blew his whistle and AB realised the ball had just carried over the crossbar. The score was 8–5 to Warmbaths Primary. His teammates swarmed around him, hugging and screaming and slapping him on the back.

Although AB's foot was stinging from the kick, he tried to hide the pain and walk normally over to his dad. The coach was shaking his dad's hand and the two men turned towards AB.

'Helluva kick, AB, helluva kick,' the coach said enthusiastically.

'Well done, son,' his father congratulated him. 'I couldn't tell if you were going to take a chance and go for it.'

'Neither could I,' said AB, 'but then it just happened.'

CHAPTER 8

A NATURAL

AB was a natural at sports. If there was a ball involved, he wanted to play, get involved, compete and be the best. But the first sport he was really serious about was tennis.

For the past year, AB had been playing in tennis tournaments around the country: the Northern Transvaal Open at Groenkloof, the Southern Transvaal Open in Johannesburg, then Bloemfontein, Durban, East London, Port Elizabeth, all the way down to Cape Town. He was seeded in the top two players for most tournaments. He enjoyed most of it, except for the twin horrors of carsickness and endless traffic jams.

'Get over here, AB, I need to talk to you,' shouted Danny Sullivan, from across the net.

'Coming, coach,' AB called, running towards the net and skipping over it.

'Not like that, AB, that's how silly injuries occur. Don't take chances for no reason, it's un-professional,' Danny reprimanded him.

AB felt sure that he would never hurt himself doing something as easy as skipping over a tennis net, but he nodded.

'How long have we been out here, today?' Danny asked him.

'Half an hour, coach. Still half an hour to go.'

'That's right. And how many balls do you think you've hit?'

'I'm not sure … maybe 400?'

'Wrong. I've been counting. In half an hour, you've hit 180 balls,' said Danny.

AB wasn't sure if that was a lot or a little, but he soon got his answer.

'Do you know how many the professionals hit? A thousand balls, every day.'

'Wow, that's a lot,' said AB.

'That's what it takes to make it to the top. Dedication, commitment and focus,' his coach told him, picking up a ball and serving it into the net. 'Listen to me, AB.' Danny put down his racket and turned to AB. 'You've got buckets of talent and you could make it in this game if you really want to.'

AB nodded, listening hard.

'But it's going to take everything you've got. You need to decide how serious you are about tennis and then go from there. Don't be fooled that it's going to be easy for you because you're naturally gifted. It's not.'

AB swallowed hard and tried to focus on what the coach was saying. He enjoyed tennis, but he wasn't sure he wanted to make it his whole life. Rugby, cricket, athletics ... they were all sports he loved. He wasn't ready to choose one of them over the rest.

After tennis practice, AB hopped on his bike and was heading home, when he saw Stoffel and Chris on their bikes, waiting for him at the school gates.

'What's up, boys?' shouted AB.

'Not much, just wanted to see if you're still in shape after all this so-called sport,' Stoffel called back.

AB laughed and realised that his friends had no idea how hard he had been working: on the court, running laps and going to the gym. He knew how fit he was. To them, fitness began and ended on the rugby pitch.

'OK, first one to the dam!' AB grinned when he saw his friends' faces light up. They all loved a challenge.

'We'll keep some Oros for you when we're chilling with our feet in the dam,' said Chris and they all laughed and turned their bikes around.

'Marks, set, go!' shouted AB and the three of them pelted off on their BMXs, whooping and laughing.

The boys knew all the dirt roads, potholes, sudden turns and tree stumps of their childhood home like an old postman knows the route he's worked for 20 years. They raced fast, up and down banks and past gardens with sprinklers and swings, purple jacaranda trees and hadedas screeching overhead.

AB pedalled faster and sped past his friends, who tried to keep up. Racing up the hill, AB

AB pedalled faster and sped past his friends, who tried to keep up.

thought about how he was no longer so nervous about playing in the big tennis games. He was also learning to play with more patience and to figure out an opponent's strengths and weaknesses, and to build each victory point by point and game by game. But something was missing.

At the top of the hill, he pulled over and turned back to look for his friends, but they were far behind. Stof was still pedalling bravely up the bank, but Chris had given up and was on his hands and knees, panting hard, at the side of the road.

AB smiled, waved and did a little victory dance. Then he whipped off his T-shirt and waded into the dam, dipping under the water and enjoying the cool sensation on his skin.

After a couple of minutes, the others came laughing and tumbling into the water, gasping in pain and relief.

'Can't take the pace, can you, boys? Maybe I need to tell coach to get serious with training,' he teased.

'It's not that, Abbas. I just took such a hit in the game on Saturday, my leg's still not right,' Chris defended himself.

'*Ja*, man, we needed you at fly-half, we would have crushed them!' Stof added.

'I know. I felt bad about missing that game.'

AB had been playing tennis in the semi-finals against an old rival, Kevin Anderson, while the rugby game was being played.

'*Ja*, it was close. We'll get them next time, though,' said Stof, and started describing a try that he had been involved in. Chris added comments, and AB listened. He really missed the feeling of working with teammates to score. At heart, he was a team player, and tennis was a lonely game.

Stoffel snuck up behind AB and dunked him under water.

'Stop daydreaming, AB!' he shouted and Chris laughed and piled in, too.

Riding home later that evening, AB noticed that the lights in Danny Sullivan's kitchen were on. He rode up to the window, knocked on the glass and waved. Danny saw him and came outside.

'Everything OK, AB?' he asked.

'Fine, coach, thanks.'

'Do you want to come in?'

AB shook his head. He needed to get back home. His mother would already be starting to get worried.

'I was just … I've been thinking about what you said earlier, about committing everything to tennis … a thousand balls a day,' said AB.

Danny nodded and waited for AB to go on.

'The thing is, I do love the game … but maybe not enough for that.'

This was hard for AB to say. When it came to sport, he tried never to give up, no matter what. And he knew that he was good at tennis. But something wasn't right.

'I understand. But what are you actually saying, AB?' Danny asked, and before AB knew he was going to say it, it all came out.

'I think I want to go back to rugby, coach. I'm sorry, but I miss teammates and tactics and working on moves together, and tennis is just … it's only me out there.'

Danny Sullivan knew the potential that AB had. He could play at Wimbledon and the Davis Cup if he wanted to, and Danny could show him the way. But he couldn't argue with what AB was saying. It was about something deeper than tennis.

Danny nodded. 'If that's what you want, AB, then it's OK with me. Go speak to your parents, and I'll ring the coach and tell him you'll be at rugby practice Monday afternoon.'

CHAPTER 9

AFFIES NEW BOYS

In the first few days of 1998, when AB was thirteen, he travelled from the small town of Warmbaths to the bustling city of Pretoria, to take up his place at the Afrikaanse Hoër Seun-skool, or Affies, as everyone called it.

Although he was hot and uncomfortable in his white shirt and grey trousers, and the hand-me-down green, yellow and red blazer that his brothers had worn before him, he was excited to be there.

'Hey you! De Villiers! Hey! Is that you?' shouted someone.

AB looked around to see a tall boy waving at him. AB nodded and jogged over. He thought that the older boy looked like he had already started shaving.

'I'm your matric for the year,' the boy said,

sizing AB up. 'What's your first name?'

'AB.'

'My name is Swanepoel but that's not important to you. You call me Master, is that clear?'

'Master?'

'Master. And I call you whatever and whenever I feel like it. Right now you don't deserve to be AB. I'll call you BA. That's the way it works at Affies. Come, let's walk.'

Swanepoel took off at a fast pace down the passageway and into the garden, heading for the assembly hall. Crowds of boys were streaming in the same direction from all over the school. The sight of all the uniforms thrilled AB; he already felt like an Affies boy.

Inside the hall, AB looked around, unsure of where to go, until he felt a finger poking him in the shoulder.

'Go join the other newbies in the front, obviously,' said Swanepoel. 'The matrics are at the back. Every year you work your way further away from the stage and Ms Cronje's flying spitballs when she's singing her favourite songs.'

AB nodded and thanked him for his help.

'Don't get the wrong idea, *laaitie*. On paper, I'm here to help you settle in, so today I'm giving you a break as it's your first day. But in reality, you're here to make life easier for me and don't forget it. I own you, BA.'

AB walked down the hall, towards the other 13-year-olds in the front. Where was he going to sit? Did he know anyone here? None of his friends from Warmbaths was at Affies. But just as he was about to slide onto the edge of a bench, AB spotted a kid he had played alongside at the South African primary schools cricket week. Was his name Francois?

A matric boy was making his way up onto the stage and the big hall was slowly falling quiet. AB made a quick decision and headed towards the boy with the familiar face.

'Move up, please, we're friends, move up,' said AB as he reached the boy, who was squeezed tightly between a big blonde boy and a boy wearing spectacles.

'No place-keeping,' said the blonde boy.

'OK, let's settle down,' shouted the head boy, pacing up and down the stage. 'Settle!'

AB felt a moment of panic. He was stuck in the middle of a pack, with no place to sit down and no-one prepared to budge.

'It's OK, come, I've got space,' the familiar-looking boy offered, and AB smiled in relief.

'Thanks,' he said as he shoved his way into the tiny gap.

'Pick up your pens and paper, boys, you're about to learn the first and most important lesson at Affies – the honour code', said the head boy, and hundreds of boys began scrabbling around in their bags for something to write with.

'You're AB, right? Batsman?' asked the boy.

'That's me. And you're Francois?'

'*Ja*, but everyone calls me Faf. At least I know one person here, now.'

'Same,' said AB.

The head boy began reading the honour code to the boys and they wrote down each word dutifully. It was a set of ideals that the Affies boys were required to live by. AB liked what it said:

45

'Strive to be helpful and serve … We believe in self-control, humility and loyalty …We respect and honour our parents and teachers …'

Finally, the head boy reached the end, and all the boys looked up in relief and stretched.

'Right, boys, let's have a great year and make it one that Affies remembers for a long, long time. Find your new classes. The bell rings in ten minutes.'

The boys all whooped and cheered.

'Except for you standard sixes. You're going nowhere. I want you each to write out the honour code a hundred times. That's your work for the morning.'

The boys sat there in stunned disbelief. A hundred times? Surely they had heard wrong. But the laughter and cackling from the rest of the school told them that this was no joke, it was what every new intake of boys at Affies faced.

Faf groaned softly and looked down at his page. One by one, the boys began writing.

'This is going to take me longer than it would to score a century against Pakistan,' said AB and

Faf started to giggle. AB laughed at Faf's crazy laugh, which only made Faf laugh more. Soon both of them were choking back howls of laughter, their shoulders shaking as they tried to write and not get caught.

CHAPTER 10

OPENING THE BATTING

The first two years at Affies passed in a blur. AB had never been busier or more challenged, and he loved every second. At first he was intimidated by all the masters and the traditions but he soon got the hang of it and, surprisingly, ended up quite liking Swanepoel.

The sporting tradition at the school was strong, which had produced legendary South African sporting stars, like Danie Visser and Johan Kriek. Some of the older boys, like Fourie du Preez and Francois Swart, were already being identified as future Springboks. Even the principal was a former Springbok fullback.

AB played some tennis matches for the school but his love for tennis had already faded. He knew that his future lay in team sports. He played hockey for a year and did quite well; but rugby was what he really wanted to be known for. Although he was shocked to find himself starting out in the Under-14F team, he worked hard. The following year he was promoted to Under-15E.

Things were different on the cricket pitch. In 2000, AB was thrilled to be chosen for the Gauteng team participating in the Coca-Cola high schools cricket week. It felt like a big break and AB was looking forward to meeting players from other schools.

'AB, good to have you here. You and me are flying the Affies flag this week,' an older boy called French greeted him in the changing room before the first game.

'Thanks French, I can't believe I'm actually here,' AB replied.

'You are. It's really happening. But don't call me French in front of the other boys. That can be an Affies secret,' French winked.

'Got it. You're captain anyway, so I'll just call you Captain.'

The coach walked into the changing room, waving a slip of paper.

'Gather round boys, gather round. I don't know you all yet but I will by the end of the week. Our first game today is against Free State, and they've got some great players,' he said. 'We're going to need to bat very deep. I'm giving the list to your captain, Francois Geldenhuys. He's from Affies and everyone calls him French.'

AB caught French's eye and laughed.

'OK boys, let's get out there and do business,' said the coach, clapping his hands enthusiastically.

French was studying the list. 'Coach. Hang on a second,' he interrupted. Everyone stopped to listen. 'You've got De Villiers batting at seven. I think he should bat higher up.'

The coach wasn't used to being challenged by schoolboys.

'There's a lot of talent in this team, Frenchie, we bat deep.'

'I agree, Coach, we do. But AB should open the batting. On this pitch, with their attack, he's the right guy …'

The room fell silent and AB felt totally awkward.

'I'm just happy to be ...' he started, but French shot him a look and the words dried up in AB's mouth.

The coach stared at French for a while, and everyone waited. Then he broke into a big grin. 'A strong captain, that's what we need on this team! Good stuff! OK, De Villiers, pad up. You're opening.'

AB's knees were shaking as he sat down to put on his pads. More than anything else in his life, he wanted to repay the faith that French had in him. He expected the captain to come over and say a few words to him, but that didn't happen and so eventually AB stood up and walked out onto the pitch.

Almost immediately, it was clear that this was a different level of cricket. Two deliveries in the first over beat the bat and narrowly missed off stump. In the next over, he had to duck to get out of the way of a delivery that would have taken his head off.

Gradually AB began to relax and remember all the things that he loved about batting. He was a fighter, his brothers had told him that a million times, and now he was planning to show that to the country.

An hour and a half later, AB pulled a ball to the boundary for four runs and saw '100' next to his name on the scoreboard. He was delighted and proud, and very relieved that he'd been able to prove to the coach that French had been right.

At the end of the week, AB was chosen to play for the South African Colts team. And it was all because of French's support. One day, thought AB, I want to be captain and give some other guy a chance to be noticed.

CHAPTER 11

THE TROUBLES

In 2001, after years of battling to impress, AB was finally being given a chance. When the rugby season had started, he was selected as fly-half for the fifth team; then a few injuries in the third team meant that he was promoted.

When he did well in a game that the second team coach happened to watch, he was promoted again. Second team was a big deal at Affies, and in his first game AB had played like a star, converting all seven kicks that he had at the posts.

The first team (the 'Wit Bulle') had just scraped to a win, and people were worried about what was going to happen when they played Hoërskool Brandwag from Uitenhage the following Saturday.

On Monday morning before class, AB's

friends were chatting about the situation in the first team.

'I heard that Potgieter wants to move to centre,' someone said.

'He'd be much better there. He's a natural 12,' agreed AB.

'You should be fly-half, AB. It's obvious.'

AB secretly agreed, but he shrugged his shoulders. 'I dunno … maybe it's too soon. I was playing fifth team last month, and now this?'

A few days later, AB met up with some friends at the school's 'radio station'. A few of the older boys had worked out a way to broadcast within a radius of about 500 metres of the school, and they would gather on weekends and make radio shows.

The previous week, between songs, they had spent quite a lot of time on air having a lively discussion about a teacher's daughter. AB thought he had been very entertaining when he described her to the listeners.

This week, all anyone wanted to talk about was the upcoming rugby match. AB had already spent so much time imagining himself in the game that he got over-excited when he told the listeners what Affies would do to Brandwag that weekend.

On the day that the team was to be announced, AB was trying hard not to fall asleep in Geography, when he heard his name being called over the intercom. He high-fived a few friends on the way out, and jogged towards the office. He had never imagined that the principal would call him in person to tell him he was in the first team.

But his fantasy crumbled when he saw the expression on the principal's face. The man staring angrily at him from the other side of the desk was not a master who felt proud of his student. AB sat down, wondering what he'd done wrong.

'Sir?'

'I've been hearing reports about your radio station from the principal of the girls' school. Apparently it reaches them,' Dr Edwards said, and waited.

'I think it does, yes,' said AB.

'They tell me you have strong opinions on

the shape of Mr Fourie's daughter's ankles. Is this true, De Villiers?'

AB gulped, unsure of what to say. 'I think … we all do have strong opinions on them, sir.'

'Are you out of your mind, boy? To put that on the radio?'

AB hadn't really thought of it like that. He had just tried to be entertaining for the listeners. He suddenly realised that his predictions about the upcoming game between Affies and Brandwag might also have offended some people, so he decided to try to explain before the principal went on.

'And when I said that we were going to beat Brandwag to within an inch of their lives, I meant beat them as in on the field … the score … You understood that, right?'

Dr Edwards slammed a ruler down on the desk. 'Good grief, De Villiers, I didn't listen to it! I didn't want to know what you said, but now I know and I have to act on that information.'

The room fell silent as they both thought about what that meant.

'That's all for now. I'll call your mother and arrange a convenient time for us to meet.'

'Yes sir. We didn't mean any harm. We were just …' AB tried to explain as he got up.

'I know. But words have consequences, AB. Tell one of the others in the radio station to come here, please.'

AB had already reached the door when he heard the worst.

'Oh, and you're banned from playing any sports until further notice,' said the principal.

'But sir, just this game … this game means everything to me this weekend.'

'How can I put an Affies boy on the field who has publicly threatened to beat up the other school? How will it make me look?'

AB's shoulders slumped. 'Not "beat up", sir. Just "beat",' he mumbled as he turned to leave.

Waiting for his mother in the car, while she spoke to the principal, was one of the scariest experiences of AB's life. He'd much rather be facing the world's fastest bowler than thinking about the conversation that was going on in the principal's office.

His mother came back to the car slowly, trying to put on a brave face, but when she slammed the door and turned to look at him, a sob came bursting out of her chest.

'You've been expelled from the boarding house for the rest of the term. You can't stay here anymore.'

AB was stunned. His home in Warmbaths was hours away from school. He could never get to school and back every single day.

'We may have to find you a new school, closer to home. I don't know what else to suggest,' she said and the tears began to flow.

Suddenly, there was a knock on AB's window and he looked up to see Dr Kriek, a well-respected teacher and first team rugby coach, signalling for him to get out of the car.

'This is a bad business, AB, I want you to know that,' he said gravely. AB nodded and looked down at his feet. He'd never felt this bad before. 'But I've seen situations like this before and trust me, it will blow over. It always does. You've just got to wait it out,' Dr Kriek continued.

'I may have to go to a new school. We live too far away from here,' replied AB.

'No son, I don't want you even thinking like that. You're an Affies boy through and through, and we'll make a plan for the rest of the term.'

AB felt better, and he tried to reassure his mother as they drove out of the school gates. After a few phone calls, they did come up with a plan. AB would stay with his Aunt Suzanne's family in Brooklyn, and take the bus to school every day with his cousin, Riaan.

AB was welcomed into their home with love and kindness. AB knew that he dare not cause any more trouble, and he worked harder than ever before, on the sports field and in the classroom, and decided to keep his opinions on ankles to himself.

CHAPTER 12

A VERY GOOD YEAR

The following year, 2002, was AB's best ever – he was the starting fly-half for every single 1st XV rugby game.

The Wit Bulle had an amazing team, with players like Pierre Spies at eighth man and Sarel Potgieter on the wing, and after 12 games they were undefeated. The upcoming big match against Grey College in Bloemfontein was all that anyone could talk about.

First team matches always drew a big crowd, but AB was stunned to see that over 14 000 people had gathered for this titanic clash. His parents had come to watch him, and AB was determined to show them he was a valuable member of the team.

The Wit Bulle got off to a great start, tackling hard and finding gaps in Grey College's defence.

The crowd roared them on and they began putting points on the board. No-one could believe it when Affies were ahead with a score of 21–0, with only five minutes left of the first half.

Then a scrum was awarded on Affies' 22-metre line and the ball was whipped back to AB. He lined up a punt and sent it sailing, but it was charged down by Grey's young superstar, Ruan Pienaar. The ball bounced kindly for Grey College and they went over for a try, to make the score 21–7 at half-time.

AB was disappointed in himself as he walked off the field. But when he nearly bumped into former Proteas captain, Hansie Cronje, talking to a Grey's parent, he forgot his disappointment. He was thrilled to be standing so close to a legend of South African cricket. When AB had been a kid, Hansie had been his hero.

Turning back to the game, AB realised that Grey College was now coming at Affies with overwhelming power and skill. By the end of the game, Grey had 46 points on the board, while Affies had not added a single point in the

AB had always dreamed about what it would be like to play there ...

second half. It was a defeat that would hurt for a long time.

The Affies boys got their season back on track the following weekend, but the result was overshadowed by the terrible news that Hansie Cronje had died in a plane crash. AB couldn't believe that he had been standing next to Hansie just a week ago and now he was dead. The whole nation was in shock.

By the end of the season, Affies had won 22 of the 23 games they played. Everyone agreed this was one of the best teams to wear Affies jerseys.

AB was selected to play for the Blue Bulls Under-18 team, and he enjoyed some magical games in the light blue uniform at the incredible Loftus stadium. Every single day, for the past few years, he had looked up at that stadium from the school fields and dreamed about what it would be like to play there – and now he had done it.

CHAPTER 13

DROPPED

Rugby was the glamour sport at school. Everyone knew who the best players were, the whole school attended big games and even the newspapers and radio reported on the scores every weekend.

AB loved rugby, and he was great at it, but by the time he reached matric in 2002 it had become clear to him that cricket was the game where he could really establish himself.

But just before the final cricket season at school began, he fell awkwardly in a rugby tackle and his elbow popped out of its socket. He was in agony for a few minutes, until the medic snapped it back into place. Although the injury wasn't serious, AB had to sit out the first half of the cricket season.

Faf du Plessis had been selected for Affies'

first team when he was only 14 years old and was the team's star player. AB made it into first team a year later, and together they formed the core of a cricket team that was a match for any schoolboy side in the country.

One sunny Highveld afternoon, Faf and AB jogged slowly around the cricket pitch, laughing about a movie that they had seen together. Every time that AB pulled slightly ahead, Faf tried to ankle-tap him so that he stumbled or fell. AB started returning the favour and soon they were stumbling around like a couple of sleepwalkers.

Across the field, they could see the rest of the team warming up and stretching before practice. Then a loud whistle burst through the air, and they saw their coach, Denis Lindsay, waving at them to come back and join the practice.

'Race you back,' shouted Faf and they took off across the field. Again AB went ahead and again Faf tried to trip him up. As AB hit full speed, Faf timed it perfectly and AB went sprawling into the grass. Both boys were still laughing as they reached the coach.

'Afternoon coach, we were just warming up with a jog,' said Faf.

Coach Lindsay didn't say anything for a while, just carried on unpacking the wickets and pads for the practice. He didn't even make eye contact.

'Coach?' said AB.

'You lads can pack your bags and go home. You're not playing on Saturday.'

'What! Why?' asked Faf angrily.

'Why? Because you don't take it seriously. Because you both think you're so valuable to the team that you don't have to practise like the rest.'

'We were jogging, coach, getting our fitness levels up,' protested AB.

Now the coach turned his full glare on them and the boys could see that he meant business. 'Is that what you call it? Laughing, tripping each other and risking injury? Running so slowly I could walk faster? That's what you call training? I don't think so. Not on my team.'

There was a stunned silence. Faf and AB just stood there, unsure what to do next. The rest of the team were dead silent, too, pretending to keep busy but listening to every word. Of course, the coach was sending a message to the whole team.

'You're both good cricketers. Who knows, one day you could be great cricketers. But your attitude stinks. When we're out here on the field, we work hard, we take it seriously, we don't goof around and risk injury. So pack your bags and get out of here … we'll see you next week.'

The coach turned and walked back to the nets. AB and Faf stood around awkwardly for a while, but then it became clear that there was no changing his mind, so they packed up and left.

Faf was fuming as they reached the hostel. AB had never seen him this cross before.

'I'm telling you, he's losing it,' said Faf. 'We did nothing wrong and now look what's happened.'

AB stopped walking and dropped his bag.

'Maybe he was right,' he muttered under his breath.

'What?' asked Faf in disbelief.

'We were messing around, Faf. In fact, we've

been cruising all season. I know I can do better. Train harder. So why haven't I been doing it?'

Faf threw his hands up in frustration.

'What's done is done. Let's move on. But that's going to be the last time a coach tells me I'm not trying my best,' AB promised, picking up his bags and dumping them in his room. 'I'm hitting the gym. See you later.'

Faf watched him go, then as AB turned the corner, he suddenly sprang into action.

'Abbas, wait, I'm coming, too!'

CHAPTER 14

READY TO GRADUATE

There were only two games left in the season, when AB heard that he had been selected to play for Northerns B Team in the provincial finals against Western Province at Newlands in Cape Town. It was a great honour, but his last two games with Affies ever were too important. Once they were gone there would be no getting them back.

The games were against Pretoria Boys High and King Edward VII School (or KES), both brilliant teams with amazing cricket programmes, and nothing in the world would make AB miss them.

It was a stormy and grey Saturday morning when the game against Pretoria Boys High got underway. The wind was howling and they could hear thunder in the distance. Affies lost the toss and were put in to bat.

When the Boys High opening bowler bowled a quick away swinger in the first over, AB followed it with his bat, got a slight touch and was caught behind by first slip. He was furious with himself. Had he given up a provincial final in Cape Town, only to sit in the stands and watch?

A few overs later, the skies opened and soaked the field. The boys ran and grabbed the covers to pull over the wicket and keep it dry, but it was too late.

After a couple of minutes of downpour, the umpires decided that there would be no chance of cricket for the rest of the day, and they rescheduled the game for two weeks later. AB was relieved that he would get another chance to bat against Pretoria Boys High, but he was still angry with himself about his performance.

The next week's match against KES was another epic encounter. The teams were very evenly matched, and the game was tight all the way through.

It all came down to the final over. KES needed seven runs off the last over with one wicket in

He lunged forward, arms out, and just got his fingers to the ball.

hand. They ticked them off in ones and twos, until they needed only three runs more from the last two balls.

AB crouched down behind the wicket in his gloves and pads, concentrating hard on the ball as the bowler released it and the batsman got a thick edge, and the ball went flying up high.

He turned hard to his right and started chasing, screaming out, 'Mine! I got it!' But it was going too fast and he had to speed up while looking over his shoulder to keep the ball in sight. He lunged forward, arms out and just got his fingers to the ball. Then it popped out of his hand and thudded to the ground.

The KES players on the side of the field whooped as the batsmen ran through for the winning runs. AB lay still on the ground, not wanting to get up and face his teammates. Two massive disappointments in the last two games of the season!

'That's cricket, AB,' said Coach Botes, as they boarded the bus to go home.

A week later, AB felt somehow different for

the rematch against Pretoria Boys High. The events of the last two games had toughened him up. He realised that if he was going to make it as a professional player, he needed to be able to bounce back from a defeat and give everything he had.

He was ready to graduate.

AB opened the batting and he was still there at the end of the day. In the last over he tried desperately to get to 200 runs, but was caught on the boundary with just a few balls to go. He had to settle for an Affies record of 196 runs, which everyone told him would last for a very long time.

Later that night, after lights out, a small group of boys grabbed a few personal belongings and torches and sneaked out of the hostel.

AB was among them. 'Quiet guys,' he whispered. 'We don't want to get detention on the last day of school.'

The boys quickly found an old spade stashed behind the work-shed and took turns to dig a deep, rectangular hole near the main gates, as quietly as they could. Finally, it was finished and they stood around panting and admiring their handiwork.

'Let's get the trunk,' someone said in the darkness and a few boys scampered off.

Waiting in the dark and silence, AB reflected on his time at Affies. He couldn't believe that it was over; the years had flown by so fast, and he had learned so much and made so many great friends. Would they all stay in touch, he wondered.

One by one, the boys each put something that they valued into the trunk. AB had brought his old school blazer and tie with him, as well as a long letter. School shoes, prefect badges and homework diaries were piled up. Last but not least, they placed a bottle of champagne in a corner of the trunk.

'What a waste of bubbly,' one of the boys complained.

'It's not a waste,' said AB. 'This is what's going to happen. None of us is going to mention the existence of this memory box to another living soul.' The boys all nodded in agreement. 'Then we're going to meet back here in exactly ten years' time. In this spot, on this day, in 2012. We'll dig up the box and drink the champagne, and it'll be perfect.'

Everyone agreed that it was a brilliant idea. They looked around for landmarks that would help them remember the spot. Then they lowered the trunk gently, filled in the hole, patted the soil down and sneaked back to bed.

As AB ran back across the cricket field, he paused at the crease and bent down to stroke the cropped grass. He was hoping that his future would see him playing on fields like this one all over the world, but he knew that the Affies field would always be his home ground.

CHAPTER 15

UNDER 19

It took some time for AB to get used to the sudden freedom when school ended. He had enrolled at the University of Pretoria to study Sports Science, but all he could think about was living life to the full and being ready for whatever opportunities came up. He practised as hard as ever, but he partied hard, too.

There was no shortage of celebration all over town. The big sporting event of 2003 was looming large – the ICC Cricket World Cup, which South Africa was hosting.

One Sunday morning when AB was back at home, the phone rang.

'AB, hi, it's Dave Nosworthy here.'

AB would have been happy to hear from the Titans coach about almost any subject, but when Dave told AB that he wanted him to play for the

Titans in a warm-up match against Canada, AB was stunned.

He managed to squeak out a 'yes' and a 'thank you' before running off to tell his family the good news. He knew Nosworthy had seen him play a few times at Affies, but he never dreamed that he would get a call-up to play for the Titans so soon. Just a few months before, he had been playing schoolboy cricket; now he was going to play against a world-class national team.

When he arrived at Centurion Park, AB felt more like a schoolboy who had come to ask his heroes for autographs than a teammate who would be playing alongside them. But a few familiar faces reassured him – Jacques Rudolph from Affies, and Martin van Jaarsveld, who had been playing against AB since they were small kids.

Despite the big occasion and the television cameras, AB settled quickly at the crease. He batted first with Jacques Rudolph and they hit a partnership of 105 before Rudolph was dismissed and Martin came to the crease.

AB powered onwards and hit a maiden century for the Titans in his first game with them, and in front of a large television audience. He was thrilled.

Later in the week, AB came back down to earth with a thump when he saw his name listed for Tukkies' second team. Playing for the Titans meant nothing; he had to prove himself at Pretoria University, just like everyone else.

Life was good, though. When he wasn't on the cricket pitch, he was out with his friends. The work that he was supposed to be doing to earn his degree was suffering, and AB felt guilty about it.

During a party, AB's phone rang and he saw that it was the Titans coach again.

'Hi, Dave, what's going on?'

'Actually, quite a lot, AB,' said Dave.

'Oh, *ja*? Like what?'

'Like I've selected you to be part of the SA Under-19 tour to England in June. If it's not going to get in the way of your studies.'

'Are you kidding?' AB felt stunned. He had forgotten that Nosworthy was not only the Titans coach, but also head coach of the Under-19 national side.

'Not at all. You've worked hard and earned your spot on the team.'

'Thank you, sir. Thank you. I'll be there, wherever and whenever you need me.'

'Great. We've got an eight-day training camp scheduled at the new High Performance Centre in Pretoria, so I'll see you there.'

The Under-19s had three Tests lined up against England, and looking around at the players assembled, AB quickly realised that international cricket was a step up from anything that any of them had played before.

There was some serious talent in their squad – players like Vernon Philander and JP Duminy were rising stars – but England had young players coming through like Alastair Cook, who forced the opposition to stay out on the field for hours when he was batting.

During the second Test, England made a monster score of over 500 runs in their first innings, and then ripped into the Proteas Under-19 top order. By lunch on the third day, the Proteas' score was 54 runs for three wickets, and they were still behind by 500 runs.

But AB had always loved a challenge; that was his favourite kind of cricket. When he had to dig deep under pressure, the game really meant something to him. Luckily, JP felt the same way. They came together when the team was down and out, and they stood their ground.

For the rest of the day, AB and JP simply refused to make any mistakes or take any chances, and they walked off the field undefeated, with a score of 166 runs for three wickets. AB had never felt prouder.

The next morning, the two batsmen worked together again to make England sweat. They played carefully, but were not afraid to punish bad deliveries, and the score ticked along while the clock ran down.

Finally, JP was out, with the score on 220 runs. JP and AB had inspired the whole team, and they carried on batting through the evening to end on a very respectable draw. It was a great fightback, and AB realised that sometimes a draw can feel like a victory, especially on the international stage.

Back at the hotel, the exhausted players quickly changed into swimming togs and met up at the hotel pool for some lunch.

'Great innings, AB,' said Big Vern Philander. 'If you can score the runs and I can take the wickets, who knows what could happen down the road for this team?'

'You know, sometimes you get that feeling,' JP remarked from where he was standing in the pool and listening to AB and Vern chat.

'Which one in particular?' asked AB.

'When you look around at your teammates and realise that, with a bit of luck, this could be a great team. A World Cup winning team. That feeling.'

'To be honest, I've had that feeling about every team I've been in, since Under-9A at Warmbaths Primary,' said AB and the others laughed. 'But seriously, I know what you're saying. This team has got it all.'

They heard excitement at the entrance to the hotel and turned to see some of the senior Proteas players arriving. The Proteas were also touring, and a couple of the players had come through with brilliant individual performances, most notably Makhaya Ntini and the captain, Graeme Smith, who had scored an incredible 259.

AB watched as Graeme Smith walked around the pool to where the Under-19s were chilling. Smith, or Biff as all his teammates called him, sat down and took off his sunglasses.

'I heard you boys put up a great fight,' said Graeme. 'Well done.'

They all mumbled thanks and nodded.

'Your innings was awesome,' AB ventured, '259 runs in a Test? Amazing!'

'Thanks. Sometimes it all just comes together,' Graeme smiled.

The younger players nodded and sat there awkwardly, not quite knowing what to say to the captain.

'So I just wanted to say hi, and tell you guys to keep up the good work. We need players like you coming through into the team. Keeps us old guys on our toes!' he said, smiling and getting up.

'That's just what we were saying,' said JP. 'Our new talent with your guys' experience? World beaters, no doubt!'

Smith gave a thumbs-up and walked back to join his teammates. The atmosphere among the Under-19s was buzzing after Smith's visit. They could clearly see the goal now, and what it was going to take to get there.

CHAPTER 16

COACHING

AB took up his guard in the nets on a chilly September morning. The fog was thick in the air and cut off the view of Table Mountain in the distance. He was alone with long-time coach Shane Gouldie, who was holding six tennis balls in his hands.

He lifted his bat and Shane started throwing the balls one by one, in quick succession. AB pulled, then drove, drove again, missed one, cut the next, missed another and finally blocked the last ball. Shane started picking up the balls, ready for another session.

'The trick is to turn off the brain here. Pure instinct. Forget about it, and just do what you do. There's no time to think,' he said, and AB agreed.

'Reaction time is everything when you're

facing a ball coming at you at 140 kilometres per hour,' continued the coach, resuming his position.

Another six balls in a row, and AB tried to just react as they came at him.

'Aaargh! Come on!' shouted AB. He was frustrated; he reckoned he had scored shots off two, maybe three, of them. His whole career, he had been able to score runs freely, when and where he wanted to. But the last few matches had seen a slump in his form, and AB had turned to Shane to help him get back on track.

Shane moved back a few paces and slowed down a little, which gave AB a fraction more time to think about getting his feet into position as he played each ball. Then it was back into defensive mode, as Shane launched the balls to bounce up high around his ears and onto his chest.

Finally, AB had earned a break. He slumped down against one of the poles holding up the nets, breathing hard.

'Tell me something, Abbas, what's the rush?' asked Shane.

'What do you mean? I'm not in a rush.'

'Really? 'Cos you always seem to be playing like there are only a few balls left to face in your last ever match.'

'I like to keep the scoreboard ticking over. It's my style,' said AB, and Shane nodded.

'That's hard to do when you're sitting back in the dressing room though, isn't it?' he commented.

'What are you trying to say, man? Just come out and say it,' said AB.

'OK, fine. I'm just frustrated by how you're playing at the moment. It's time to get back to the basics. You don't have to score off every ball and break records every single game!' replied Shane, and AB could see his frustration.

'So you think I'm not scoring runs because I'm trying too hard and showing off?' asked AB.

'Not at all. You're just doing what's always worked for you.'

'Exactly. It's always worked for me. Why should I change?'

'Because it's stopped working, AB. You need

to adjust. Think of Tiger Woods rebuilding his whole swing from the ground up when it stopped working for him.'

'Wow,' said AB. 'I didn't realise I'm that bad.'

'That's not what I'm saying,' said Shane. 'I just think you need to slow down, is all. Play the ball that's in front of you, on its merits. Instinctively.'

AB nodded, got up. He could do that. He took up position again, and so did Shane.

'You know I think you could be one of the all-time greats, don't you?' said Shane.

'Bowl!' ordered AB, and Shane threw six balls harder and faster than before.

AB's mind switched off and he just flowed through each delivery; blocking a few, driving a couple, and even leaving one that he didn't want to touch.

Shane whooped and clapped.

'Nice, AB, nice. That's what I'm talking about!'

'That's the best reaction I've ever got for just leaving a ball,' said AB.

Shane laughed. 'That's all you have to do

sometimes. Just take your time out there and you'll see … you'll be back to scoring runs like it's the easiest thing in the world.'

CHAPTER 17

TURNING PRO

Good things come in threes. So the next time AB's phone rang and he saw that it was Dave Nosworthy, he felt a tingle of excitement. Previous calls from Dave had meant that AB had played for the Titans against Canada and, a few weeks later, in the Under-19 national team. Both experiences had been wonderful. What would Dave's phone call bring this time?

'Hello,' said AB.

'Hi AB, what are you up to?'

'Just trying to catch up on my studies at Tuks,' he replied, and gave an embarrassed chuckle. 'I'm quite far behind.'

'I'm not surprised. You've been busy,' said Dave. 'And I think you might be about to get even busier.'

AB said nothing.

'I've spoken to the board and management, and everyone's agreed, we'd like to offer you a Titans contract for the 2003/2004 season.'

AB put down the phone on the couch and punched the air wildly for five seconds. Then he got back to the phone.

'Sure, Dave, that sounds great. Thank you,' he said, trying to sound calm.

'It's only a junior contract but it's a start and it gets you into the system. R5 000 a month,' continued Dave.

AB dropped the phone onto the couch again and did a little dance around the room.

'AB?' said Dave.

'Sorry Dave, bad connection, but that all sounds great. I'll call you back when I've got better reception.'

AB hung up quickly, before letting out a whoop and clenching his fists. This was it, he was turning professional. To play cricket for money would change everything. And he would be a Titan.

But what about his studies? He felt a pit in

his stomach, and realised that it was decision time. Was he going to carry on studying Sports Science? He didn't love it, but studying had seemed like the realistic, grownup thing to do.

First, AB decided to call his uncle Chris, and speak to him about the money and what he should do with it. Five thousand rand wasn't much, but he knew that the amount a professional was paid could increase quickly.

After he had spoken to his uncle, he felt calmer. Now he should call his parents and tell them.

His mother answered, out of breath. He could picture her running to the old-fashioned phone in the hallway from somewhere in the house. She was pleased to hear from him, but she had something baking in the oven, so AB waited for his dad to get on the phone, and told him the news. Then he had to wait while his dad ran back to the kitchen to tell his mom.

When his dad finally got back on the line, AB explained how worried he was about his studies and how things weren't going very well, academically. His dad listened and said nothing for a while after AB had finished. He could hear his mother speaking quietly in the background.

'Well, son, of course it's totally up to you, but if you decide that you need to focus on your cricket then that's fine with us,' his dad said eventually.

His mother grabbed the phone. 'You can always go back and study later,' she interrupted.

'Thanks, ma,' said AB. 'I think, maybe, I will tell Tukkies that I can't carry on. Not now, anyway.'

AB felt lucky to have such supportive parents, and to have had so many good coaches and captains along the way. Still, he felt a new weight on his shoulders. Everyone believed in him and expected great things. It was time to show what he could do.

AB's professional career started off with a four-day game against Western Province in Cape Town. The Titans travelled down together, and AB started getting to know his new teammates. Dale Steyn, a young bowler, was making his debut alongside AB. Fast, strong, aggressive and controlled, Dale had all the qualities of the greats.

In that first game, AB managed to record half-centuries in both his innings. A week later, the team made the short drive to the Wanderers Stadium in Johannesburg for a second four-day game.

Fortune continued to smile on AB, who managed another two half-centuries in succession: four half-centuries in a row since turning pro. With every passing day, he felt more at home as a professional cricketer.

But AB was smart enough to know his luck couldn't last, and true enough, it didn't. The next game against Border produced the humiliating grand total of zero. That was followed by 17, which wasn't much better.

Still, he was playing well enough to earn another call-up to the Under-19 Proteas team to travel to India. When AB saw JP and Faf were also going, he was even more pleased that he was finally going to the 'cauldron' of international cricket.

CHAPTER 18

LEAVING HOME

'Life comes at you pretty fast,' thought AB, as he watched *Ferris Bueller's Day Off* on the plane. It was late at night and most of the people around him were sleeping, but AB was wide awake, trying to make sense of this new phase in his life.

A few days ago, Dave had asked him to stay behind after a meeting.

'What do you think about Carrickfergus?' asked Dave, sitting back and waiting.

AB knew he was being tested. He didn't have a clue who Dave meant, and imagined that Carrick was a player that Dave wanted to sign up to the team.

'He's impressive,' said AB, trying to play it cool.

Dave packed out laughing. 'Carrickfergus is not a player, AB, it's a place. A team, in Northern

Ireland, and they're looking for an overseas player.'

In the dark aircraft, AB smiled at the memory. He had spoken about it with his parents and his coaches and they had all thought it was a good idea for a 20-year-old to go overseas and spend some time learning about life. So here he was, on a plane to Northern Ireland, ahead of their first game against the Belfast Harlequins.

He turned the movie off, closed his eyes and tried to get some rest, but his mind kept whizzing around. How good would his team be? Where was he going to stay? And how did people get laundry done in a tiny Irish coastal town in the middle of nowhere?

Realising that he was definitely not going to sleep, AB turned the screen on again and got back to Ferris Bueller and his crazy adventures.

At the airport, AB spotted a young red-haired guy who was waiting to collect him. They piled all his stuff into a beaten-up old Volvo, and then they were off, charging up the M5 from Belfast.

'What's the rush?' asked AB and laughed uneasily as the car overtook a truck and sped up to the next intersection. The driver, Connor, checked his watch and grimaced.

'We should be OK, but I don't want to take any chances,' he replied, and AB nodded.

'Where are we going?'

The driver looked at him like he was an idiot.

'To the cricket ground. The game is supposed to start at 11 and they texted me that we're in to bat first.'

'Today? The first game is today?'

The driver nodded and they fell silent. Then after a few moments both of them packed out laughing.

'I don't even have any clean whites with me. I need to do laundry. I thought it was next Saturday,' said AB.

'No ways, mate, this is not one of those fancy teams. There's no physio and light rubdown waiting for you on the side. There's just a big, fast West Indian waiting to chuck a ball at your head,' and they both laughed again.

The car pulled up outside the cricket ground and AB grabbed his bat and fished his boots out of his luggage. Inside the changing room, he was given a fresh set of whites and told to pad up, as he was going in third. He was beginning to regret watching movies all night, but this was no time to start complaining.

He sat down to take a few deep breaths and compose himself, when he heard a cheer from the stands and a knot formed in his stomach. 'Life comes at you pretty fast,' he muttered to himself before he got up and walked out onto the field to show what he could do.

'Hey, I'm Barry Cooper,' said the other batsman, and they bumped gloves. AB thought he heard a Kiwi accent from his teammate.

'Nice to meet you. AB de Villiers.'

'Take it easy out here. The wicket can surprise you if you're not careful. And Ijaz knows how to get a real turn from it.'

'Ijaz Ahmed, the great Pakistani?' asked AB, remembering how often he'd watched the legend play for Pakistan. Barry shook his head.

'Not that one, thank goodness. But this guy means business, too.'

AB lifted the ball over the bowler's head for six.

AB took up his guard and waited for the first ball. Ijaz bowled and AB tried to drive him back over his head. The ball spun away and he mistimed it, but luckily it popped up and fell just short of mid-off. Barry shot him a dirty look from the other end, and AB decided that maybe he should listen to his advice.

The next time Ijaz came in to bowl, AB felt ready and he lifted the ball back over the bowler's head for six. Then the next ball he did it again, and started to relax and enjoy himself, although he was exhausted and uncomfortable in the borrowed clothes.

Ultimately, AB finished with 85 runs off 82 balls and Carrick won the game by six wickets.

Lying in bed that night, AB finished off his toasted cheese sandwich and realised that he had better learn to cook. Luckily, he was staying with Barry Cooper and they already felt like old friends. There was nothing like sharing a good innings to cement a friendship.

CHAPTER 19

A RUN-IN WITH THE COACH

After three months in Northern Ireland, AB felt like a changed person. He had learned how to look after himself and what life on the road was like. It wasn't easy, but he had grown up a lot.

He had also scored plenty of runs and was feeling more comfortable than ever at the crease. He was the first Carrick player to score a double century when he made 223 runs not out against Cliftonville, and he followed that up with two hundred more runs a week later.

AB felt ready for a bigger challenge on a bigger stage, so when was selected for the South African A side to tour Zimbabwe, he said a sad farewell to his new Carrick friends and rushed back to join a team that was brimming with talent.

It had been a while since he had played with Hashim Amla, Neil McKenzie, Ashwell Prince and Paul Adams. He had improved a lot in Ireland but now he realised that everyone had improved; the whole standard had gone up a level.

'Gather round, boys,' said Ray Jennings, former South African wicketkeeper and now coach. 'We've got a lot of work to do. You do realise you're one step from the top, right? There's no more working things out, slowly improving … this is it. A few good games, some wickets and a big innings and you'll reach the point that you've all been dreaming about since you were a five-year-old.'

The guys all chuckled. They knew exactly what Ray was talking about. After the team talk he got them to line up in a semi-circle, then selected a bat and a brand new ball from the pile.

'Commitment, gentlemen, commitment – that's the only thing that makes a difference at this level,' he said, and drove the ball towards the wall of players, who instinctively jumped out of the way. 'Stop the thing!' shouted Ray. 'Whatever it takes!'

He smashed another one and Ashwell Prince

bravely stuck out a leg, then yelped as it hit him on the inner thigh. The next shot saw Albie Morkel diving and getting a hand to a rocket disguised as a ball.

As the practice wore on, the players became covered in bruises, but it forged them into a team. They felt like they had been through a war together.

Walking off the field, AB couldn't help thinking that Ray Jennings knew how to get the best out of his players. He had heard that Ray was tough, but AB had really enjoyed the experience and wanted to do well for his coach.

The tour against Zimbabwe went well, so AB was surprised to find out that he had been dropped for the last match. He wasn't sure what to make of it, but was relieved to rejoin the team for a pair of four-day games against New Zealand.

On the first day of the first match, the Kiwis batted first and made a respectable 284 runs. AB came back to the cricket ground on the second day determined to do some big things and cement his place in the team.

He started well and felt that he had the measure of the bowlers and the pitch. A cut to square leg, a solid drive and a few pulls over the boundary saw AB racing to 30 runs off just 25 balls.

Things went well until the ninth over, when a ball from Chris Martin moved away from him and he tickled it into the hands of the wicketkeeper. He was disappointed but felt that 43 runs was a solid enough contribution.

That night, he got a message that there was a team meeting before play the next day and everyone had to be there early. AB was expecting one of Ray's famous pep talks, but things started to feel a little different when Ray wouldn't even make eye contact.

'De Villiers! What the hell were you thinking, man? This is your chance to explain it.'

AB was stunned and bewildered. But the problem soon became crystal clear.

'Going out there like you haven't a care in the world,' said Ray. 'Just playing free and easy, like we don't have three more days of cricket to get through … Oh no, for you it's all fun and games …

Good times, right? Good times!' Ray paused to stop himself from getting too worked up.

The rest of the team sat quietly, like a losing team of Under-11Cs. AB felt as though everyone was silently sliding along the benches away from him. It was time to be brave.

'I was feeling it, coach. Scoring quickly. I nearly …' he started, but stopped when Ray slammed his hand down hard on the wall.

'Listen to me closely … You can finish this game today, but you'll never play in a team of mine EVER AGAIN!' shouted Ray.

'It's OK, coach, he's got the message,' said the captain, Ashwell Prince.

Ray stormed out and after a few moments, the team all got up and went to get themselves ready. AB sat there in shock; he couldn't move a muscle.

His whole life he had played aggressively and tried to score off every ball. And it had always worked for him, despite some obvious ups and downs. Why was this different, and what did it mean for his career that the coach of the A-team would never pick him for another match?

He was devastated and the rest of the game passed in a blur.

AB returned home, and after a few weeks he felt like the tongue-lashing had never happened. He was playing well for the Titans, and felt a new sense of responsibility for the team. Somehow, over the last few months, he had started caring less about his own performances and more about what was best for the team.

But then his worst nightmare came true, when Ray Jennings was appointed head coach of the Proteas team for the upcoming Test series against England. Ray's comments came flooding back into AB's memory and left him feeling dejected.

So his jaw nearly hit the floor a few days later, when Haroon Lorgat, who was in charge of selecting the national team, told him that he had been selected for the first Test against England! For a second, he thought Ray must have been replaced as head coach, but that was not the case. He was about to play for his country against England, under Ray Jennings.

CHAPTER 20

THE FIRST TEST

Arriving to join the Proteas team ahead of the first Test was an experience that AB would never forget. It was the summer of 2004 and AB was just a few months away from his 21st birthday. Once again, he was making a debut with the fearsome Dale Steyn, and alongside his old friend and teammate Jacques Rudolph.

This was the big league; world-class Test cricket against a tough opponent, with a long history of epic battles between them.

Driving towards the High Performance Centre at Tukkies, AB decided that the best thing to do would be to keep his head down and not attract too much attention; just work hard, be respectful and show that he was a team player. It was going to be the first time he'd seen Ray Jennings in a few months, and he wanted to show the coach how much he had changed.

'First to arrive and last to leave,' he muttered, as he pulled up in the parking lot and headed for the gym.

The first week with the national team was intense. From training in the gym to net practice, strategy sessions and even psychological coaching, everything was bigger, better and faster. AB worked harder than ever before, and he slowly got used to being around his idols and treating them like normal people.

At the end of a gruelling week, the squad flew down to Port Elizabeth to make final preparations for the big game. AB sat next to Dale Steyn on the plane.

'Remember last year, when we made our debuts for the Titans,' said AB.

'*Ja*, I can't shake you off my tail,' joked Dale.

'Please, it's because of me that you're here,' replied AB.

'How so?'

'You need a good batsman to bowl at. It's

excellent batsmen like me that help you up your game,' AB laughed.

'I suppose. Although most of the time you don't even see the balls I bowl at you.'

They both grinned and called it a truce as the air hostess explained the safety procedures for the flight.

In the hotel, AB lay awake long into the night, going over and over his plan for the game, and what he knew about the bowlers.

The next morning, his parents called him to say that they'd be in the stands cheering him on. AB was delighted, although it made the butterflies in his stomach worse.

The stadium was filling up as the bus arrived, and AB thought back to the first time he'd ever been to a Test match. It felt like a million years ago. He saw a familiar face outside the dressing room: Derick Kuün, his old Affies teammate and an excellent sportsman. Derick greeted most of the players as they got off the bus, but AB knew that he was there for him.

'You made it!' said AB.

'Told you I would, didn't I?' Derick laughed.

'Part Two of our plan, right?'

'Exactly. Remember, we said we'd win the *Beeld* Trophy at school …'

'… And we did,' AB finished Derick's sentence.

'And we said when one of us made our international debut, the other would be there. So here I am,' said Derek and they high-fived.

'De Villiers!' roared Ray Jennings suddenly from the dressing room door. 'This is not a Hollywood red carpet! Get in here.'

AB realised he was the last one left in the parking lot and rushed inside.

Ray worked the team hard before the warm-up, and AB was already baking in the Eastern Cape sun when the captain, Graeme Smith, won the toss and decided they would bat. This was it! AB was about to open the batting for South Africa alongside Graeme Smith.

He padded up in a daze, barely hearing what anyone was saying to him. Luckily, the captain was there to calm his nerves. Smith took one look at AB and understood that he was going through a lot. As they walked out onto the field, he spoke to AB.

'Take a look around, mate. Soak it up. There's only one first time.'

AB glanced around and took a deep breath.

'They're going to come at you hard, but you can handle it. And just ignore all the chirping. Be thankful it's not the Aussies for your first Test match.'

AB nodded, but found that his voice had deserted him. He was grateful that Smith would be facing the first few balls.

But on the third ball, Smith edged one to the wicketkeeper and was caught, which left the Proteas at nil for one. AB felt the pressure mounting, but was relieved to see his old friend Jacques Rudolph coming to the wicket.

Steve Harmison was ranked the number one bowler in the world. AB set his mind to surviving the first few deliveries, while he got the measure of Harmison. Finally, after what seemed like hours, a ball came that was slightly wider of the wicket and AB sent it for four. The next one was similar and AB smashed it past a diving cover point for four more.

'Hey, this isn't too hard,' thought AB, but then he caught himself and remembered how Ray wanted him to play for the team and not get too loose. So he tightened things up again and took his time, reminding himself that he was facing the number one bowler in the world.

Slowly, Jacques and AB started building a respectable score, and AB was thrilled when his first ever Test innings produced a partnership of 50 runs. But the English were fierce and bowler Andrew Flintoff was doing all sorts of things with the ball.

A few minutes later, Flintoff got a ball to nip back off the seam and AB played and missed. He wasn't too worried; he thought it had gone too high, but the umpire had other thoughts. The fielders appealed, the umpire's finger went up and AB found himself walking back to the stands after only scoring 28 runs.

Still, the whole team performed well and managed a very respectable 337 runs for the first innings. Out in the field on the second day, AB worked hard, going for everything and chasing down balls to the boundary. He even managed to hold on to a screaming catch at point to get rid of Andrew Strauss, as Strauss was building on a massive score of 126 runs.

The English batsmen were relentless and built a really big score of 425 runs, then kept South Africa under pressure. AB was caught and bowled by Matthew Hoggard with his score on 14 runs.

He watched the rest of the innings from the dressing room as the batsmen fell regularly. England only needed to get a total of 142 runs to win, and they reached it for the loss of only three wickets.

AB was disappointed to lose his first Test match, but at least he had got it out of the way and hadn't let the team down.

In the second Test at Kingsmead in Durban, Ray Jennings and Graeme Smith decided to drop AB down to bat at seven. He was happy to do whatever the team needed, but worried that it was a demotion.

'AB, you're also keeping wicket today,' Smith winked at AB, which made him feel better.

The game started off well and the bowlers kept England on the back foot. After a few great sessions, the visitors were out for 139 and the Proteas went in to bat. AB watched as Jacques Kallis gave a batting masterclass and scored 162, to help the team reach a total of 332 runs.

But the advantage that the Proteas were feeling gradually started to fade as the English openers crafted a huge partnership. The Proteas needed something big to happen.

When Marcus Trescothick edged a ball down low, AB threw himself to his right and somehow managed to take a brilliant catch. His teammates swarmed all over him and celebrated wildly. But England kept playing well and their second innings ended with a massive total of 570 runs.

'We're batting to save the game today, boys! This is a defensive day so I don't want to see anything stupid or flashy. Be patient, play for each other,' Smith told them on the morning of the last day. AB could feel Ray Jennings's eyes boring into his neck from behind.

Just before lunch, three more wickets fell in quick succession and the Proteas were stunned. One minute they were on 170 runs after five overs, and then a few overs later they were sitting at 183 for seven. Nobody said anything as AB clattered through the dressing room and out onto the field. They all knew that he knew what was expected of him.

At the other end of the pitch was Shaun Pollock, as great a batsman as he was a bowler. They nodded at each other, then got down to business … ball by ball, over by over and session by session, AB and Shaun fended off an increasingly desperate attack by the English team.

The light was fading, but so were the bowlers and the tension crackled in the air.

'Did I ever tell you that you were playing in the first Test match I ever saw live?' AB asked, as they met in the middle of the pitch between overs.

'Abbas! Are you trying to make me feel old?' joked Shaun and AB shook his head.

'Let's just hang in there. We've got this,' AB replied.

AB's 50 came up after 108 minutes and 87 balls, but he was so focused on saving the game for the team that he barely realised he'd scored his first Test half-century.

The light was fading fast and finally the English got a breakthrough. AB and Shaun misunderstood each other, and Pollock was run out. One wicket left to go.

Makhaya Ntini came to the wicket. The English team were alive again, sniffing victory in the air, but Makhaya and AB didn't give them an inch. Makhaya was afraid of nothing. He loved the challenge and managed to score 16 quick runs off ten balls.

After what seemed like forever, the umpires checked their light meters and called an end to the game. The Proteas had hung on to scrape an important draw against England that kept the series alive.

AB collapsed back in the dressing room and someone shoved a beer into his hand. He opened his eyes to see the coach, Ray Jennings, standing above him and beaming with pleasure.

'I'm so proud of you today, AB, so proud.' said Ray.

'Thanks a lot, coach.'

'The old AB would have been unable to resist attacking some of those balls. But you didn't. You stayed with the plan and played for the team. You're a fighter.'

AB sat up and clinked his can against the coach's, as the rest of the team raised their glasses. 'On to the next one, boys!' shouted Herschelle Gibbs, and everyone cheered. AB felt like he was really part of the team.

CHAPTER 21

CENTURION

If AB thought that Test cricket was going to be easy, the next few Tests in the series swept those ideas away. He was finding runs hard to come by and began to wonder if he was going to be dropped.

Mark Boucher was back in the team to keep wicket, so AB was relying on his own performance with the bat at number six to stay in the team. He felt like he was just living from day to day.

Then, in the warm-up before the second innings of the fourth Test, Graeme Smith took a knock to the head and had a minor concussion. AB was promoted back up the batting order and was assigned to open the batting with Herschelle Gibbs.

AB knew this was a big opportunity to show

his skills as an opener, but he was nervous and unsure. When he was dismissed for only three runs, he was furious with himself. He had scored above 20 runs just twice in four games; it wasn't good enough and he was convinced that he would be dropped at the end of the series if he didn't come right.

AB decided that the fifth and final Test of the series was going to make or break his career. He was pleased that the game was being played at SuperSport Park in Centurion. It was a ground that he knew well and it reminded him of the hundreds of games he had played all over the Highveld.

But the first day brought more frustration; long, soaking rain with cold winds whipped the field and showed no sign of clearing up. Play was abandoned on Day One.

The next day, AB learned that he would open again with Herschelle and Graeme Smith would bat at number five.

AB was determined to make his mark, even though the weather conditions favoured the bowlers and he was low on confidence. He toughed out some difficult overs and then began to settle.

Runs gathered behind his name like moths around a flame, and AB breathed a sigh of relief when he reached 50. After searching the faces of the crowd for a while, AB saw his dad in the stands with his arms raised, clapping hard.

As he got into the 90s, AB was lucky to have Jacques Kallis batting alongside him. One of the all-time cricket greats, Jacques had been in this position hundreds of times.

'Keep going, AB. Don't rush it,' Jacques advised AB. 'Just do what you do well.'

Then AB swung a low ball too early, looping it up over mid-wicket. The ball dropped agonisingly close to Michael Vaughan, who dived. Running for a single, AB saw the anxiety on Jacques' face, and then relief as the ball bounced safely on the turf.

But AB was stuck on 92 runs and desperate to reach the century. He impulsively kneeled and tried to sweep a slower ball away. The ball hit the pad and AB was out LBW. He was dev-astated as he walked off. What had he been thinking?

Then it was the final innings, and a last chance to make that century. After their innings, the English team had reached a strong position of 359 runs. The South African team realised the game would be almost impossible to win. They were still going to be behind 2–1 in the series.

Maybe because victory was now out of South Africa's grasp, AB played more fluidly, working hard for himself and his partner, running quick singles and testing the opposition. In what felt like minutes he was back in the 90s, and this time there was no stopping him.

A short ball was dispatched over mid-wicket for six and AB was on 98 runs. In came Simon Jones, bowling wide outside off stump. This time, AB knew it was coming. He wasn't worried; it was just another ball in another game. He leaped onto his back foot and cut with force, safely past cover and to the boundary for four: 102 not out – he had made it!

He lifted his bat and acknowledged the crowd. Even the English players were applauding. It had been a long, tough tour and the players from both sides had developed great respect for each other.

When AB looked up at the scoreboard and saw the three digits behind his name, he was filled with emotion. A century for South Africa was a big contribution for his team and his coach. It was a proud moment for his parents and friends, and all the coaches who had helped him get here.

Jacques walked over and bumped fists with him.

'Welcome to the club, Abbas! Take your time, enjoy the moment – then let's get back to work.'

AB looked around, captured the memory, then turned back to the crease and got ready to face the next ball.

POSTSCRIPT

In the ten years after his debut in the 2004/2005 season, AB played 106 more Test matches, scoring 8 074 runs including 21 centuries, with an average of about 50 runs per innings.

The trunk buried on the school grounds still hasn't been opened; to allow everyone to be there, the friends have agreed to delay the occasion until 2022, 20 years after they left Affies.

SOURCES

De Villiers, AB. 2016. *AB: The Autobiography.* Johannesburg: Pan Macmillan South Africa.

https://www.youtube.com/watch?v=HK6B2da3DPA

https://successstory.com/people/abraham-benjamin-de-villiers

http://www.espncricinfo.com/southafrica/content/player/44936.html

http://www.espncricinfo.com/series/14925/scorecard/64116/South-Africa-vs-England-1st-Test/

http://www.howstat.com/cricket/Statistics/Matches/MatchScorecard_ODI.asp?MatchCode=0796

CLASSROOM ACTIVITIES

ORAL ACTIVITIES

1. Using Chapter 8 (A Natural), create a short play. The characters are: Danny (the coach), AB, Chris and Stoffel. There are four scenes: on the cricket ground, on bicycles to the dam, at the dam, and in Danny's house. Decide who will play which role, and use the dialogue in the chapter as your script. Plan your props, practise your play, and perform it for the class. (You could also choose just one of the scenes and create a shorter play.)

2. Put the events in Chapter 11 (The Troubles) in the order that they actually happened in AB's life, and retell this chapter in your own words. (Clue: The first bullet is the correct start to the events.) Imagine a different ending to the chapter, and include it in your story.

ORAL ACTIVITIES

- AB entertains listeners by making comments about a teacher's daughter on the 'radio station'.
- AB is called to the headmaster's office, and imagines he will be told exciting news about promotion to the first team.
- AB's friends talk about the first rugby team and say that he should be fly-half.
- The headmaster is furious with what AB has said on the 'radio station' and bans AB from playing any sport.
- The headmaster calls AB's mother to the school.
- AB goes to stay with his aunt and her family.
- AB broadcasts his opinion on the 'radio station' on the upcoming rugby match between the 'Wit Bulle' and Hoërskool Brandwag from Uitenhage.
- AB decides to work hard and keep out of trouble.
- AB is expelled from the boarding house for the rest of the term.

3. Do a class survey. Interview your classmates to find out whether they like soccer, cricket, rugby or tennis the most. Write a questionnaire of about five questions and record their answers. Create a bar graph to show the results.

4. In Chapter 5, AB watches the first Cricket World Cup that South Africa played in, and in Chapter 6, he watches Wimbledon tennis on television. Choose one of the topics (Cricket World Cup or Wimbledon tennis), research it, and give a speech of two or three minutes to the class.

5. Study the pictures in chapters 1 and 18 (pages 7 and 98). Choose one picture, and use the information in the chapter to make up a cricket commentary that describes that moment in the game. Present your commentary to the class.

WRITTEN ACTIVITIES

In the activities below, remember to follow the writing process:
- Brainstorm your ideas.
- Write a first draft.
- Revise and edit your draft, correcting grammar and spelling mistakes.
- Write a neat final draft.

1. Read chapters 2 and 4, and write a description of AB when he was in junior school. Use what he says and does to help you. In Chapter 2, AB is called a 'fighter', and in Chapter 4 he is called a 'trickster'. In what ways was he these things as a child?

2. Pretend you are AB and write a diary entry about your first day at Affies (Chapter 9). Describe what happened and how you felt about it, for example:

- how you felt about wearing the uniform
- what you think of Swanepoel
- what happened in the school hall
- your new friend
- how the rest of the school treated the new boys
- how you feel about being at the school
- what you hope will happen in the future.

3. Write a sports report for the Warmbaths Primary school magazine on the rugby game between Kruger Park Primary and Warmbaths Primary (Chapter 7). You can add your own details to the report.

4. Do you think that Coach Lindsay was correct to punish AB and Faf by dropping them from the next game and sending them home from practice? Write a paragraph in which you say what you think about the coach's decision, and explain why you think so. Convince your reader that the boys should or should not have been punished.

AUTHOR'S NOTE

The events in this book about AB de Villiers are based on fact. However, I have taken creative licence in certain scenes with dialogue and some detail in the interests of creating a story that is entertaining and fun for young readers. I have tried to stay true to the character of my subject, based on the known facts.

ALSO AVAILABLE IN THE
ROAD TO GLORY
SERIES

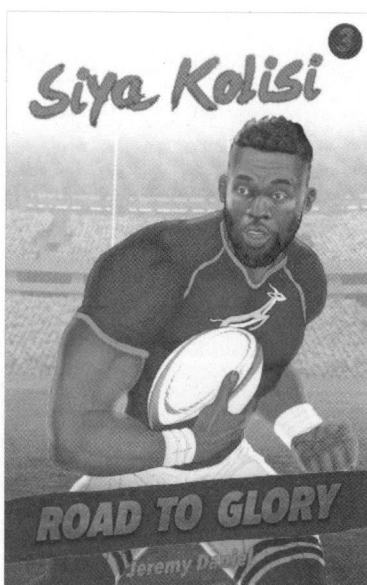